BRIDGET E. PARK

growing young

A MEMOIR OF GRIEF

ISBN: 1490416056
ISBN 13: 9781490416052

Library of Congress Control Number: 2013910763
CreateSpace Independent Publishing Platform
North Charleston, South Carolina

This book is dedicated to my brother, Austin.
Not only were you my brother, but my hero, friend, and idol.

Loved by many, forgotten by none.

Acknowledgements
A special thank you to Emilio, my family and friends who encouraged me to write this book, those who helped me in my journey of grieving, and Tamara Leigh, family friend and author of <u>The Unveiling</u> *and many other books, for all your help and support. Thank you Mom and Dad for always inspiring me and encouraging me to follow my heart and to chase my dreams. I love you!*

contents

numb

The shock of a death is like the shock of hitting cold water. The chill starts at your toes and, inch by aching inch, travels upward. Once it reaches your brain, you go numb. So numb you can't feel anything. But it doesn't last.

I was twelve years old when I lost my brother, barely old enough to know what death was beyond something terrible that happened to other people. Like many who have older siblings, I looked up to Austin who outranked me by two years. He was a scholar, an athlete, and a leader. He was my idol.

We grew up in a Catholic ranching family and were raised with horses, cattle, and a strong work ethic. My great grandfather built our family business. He developed one of the best golf courses in the nation, which hosts a nationally televised celebrity tournament each year.

My dad grew up on a ranch with his four siblings. After graduating high school, he pursued and was awarded a degree in business and agriculture. Later, he opened his own business as a financial advisor that allowed him to help others manage their money and buy stocks. He is a devoted father, a successful financial consultant, and a dedicated rancher and landowner.

As a family of four, Austin and I were the only children, so we depended on each other to fulfill the role of playmate. We played in the field, on our swing set, and rode our tricycles in our neighborhood. To entertain ourselves, sometimes we made contraptions from simple materials. Sometimes we had help. Once, our dad made us a water balloon slingshot that launched water balloons fifty feet into the air. Austin and I took turns in the field trying to catch a balloon, which always resulted in a good dousing.

My parents have told the story that when Austin was two and I was only a few months old, they heard a scream and followed it to their bedroom. My mom dropped the telephone and my dad dropped his beer at the sight that greeted them. My brother was dangling me upside down by one foot above our parents' bed and I had stickers all over my face. That started our bond.

Naturally, siblings are born with an extra sense that connects them. No matter how many fights, arguments, or brawls, this bond is one of a kind. A parent or friend cannot replace that bond. As we grew older, our bond grew stronger despite typical sibling behavior that included, but was not limited to, stealing one another's crayons and hogging the bathroom before school. At the end of the day, no matter what, we always had each other.

The small country town in which we lived was beautiful in the fall. In the fall of 2008, the fields were still as green as ever and the trees were shaking off all their leaves. The mountains surrounding the valley on all sides were topped with snow and dotted with pine trees. I was in middle school and my brother was a freshman at a small high school in Northern Nevada. He was fourteen years old, though he looked nearer seventeen with his stubble and muscular arms.

Because it was such a small town, all the grades were under one roof. This meant it was hard for my brother to avoid me. Naturally, he acted too cool for me, which I kind of expected. Austin was the freshman class president, a starter on the football team, and everyone's friend. He carried a constant a smile on his face and didn't hesitate to greet someone in the hallway. I was a shy, seventh grade girl who hid in oversized sweatshirts and sometimes wondered if I had been adopted. Attending the same school as my brother was a different story every day. Some days we got along, other days, not so well. But when we came home, we acted civil—for a little while, at least. Often, his older friends crushed on me. That's when I saw Austin's rare protective side.

In November of 2008, it was the end of the high school football season and the beginning of basketball season. My brother had long, lanky arms and he was built sturdy. Being a well-rounded athlete, he could easily join any sport and fit right in. He had never played basketball before but, living in a small town, you were expected to play. Otherwise, there would hardly be a team. My parents had a basketball court installed at our house, and every day after school, I would see Austin outside shooting and dribbling. I often watched him until I couldn't see him anymore because of the sun lowering behind the mountains. He worked hard every day and easily outdid everyone at the first practice of the season.

One Saturday, November 29, 2008, my dad gathered us to "clean up" our property, a fairly regular occurrence. Austin and I were accustomed to awakening to our dad telling us to be ready in five minutes, but we always managed to push it to ten. We had just been given our steers for 4H and I had named mine Herfy. It was to be my first time taking a steer to the livestock show since, previously, I had taken lambs.

"Bridget," my dad said, "steers are ten times bigger than you are. Don't be afraid if you have to jerk him around to gain control." I grabbed hold of the halter that would help me control Herfy, but his only reaction was to tilt his head and look at me with big eyes and long, batty lashes. It was different for Austin. When he grabbed his steer's halter, all hell broke loose. The steer ran and Austin countered by digging his heels into the dirt while my dad ran to the rescue. Meanwhile, Herfy licked my hand. Herfy and I became something like "pen pals." When Herfy laid down in his stall, I often joined him and placed my head on his belly, resting when I was supposed to be mucking.

Austin washing his steer "Moe."

The day dragged on. When, finally, the endless grind of pulling weeds, mucking stalls, and other assorted chores was at an end, we faced the next obstacle of repairing our horse trailer. I have so many memories associated with this worn out trailer. Once, my dad and I found a calf stuck in frozen manure that would not make it if we didn't intervene. We broke through the icy manure and carried the baby into the trailer where I put my jacket on it and kept him warm until we could get him to the calving barn and stabilize him.

The trailer was nearly ten years old, and we had always had issues with the tailgate lights. I was assigned the job of sitting in the truck and turning it on and off. My dad and brother were behind the trailer testing the lights. On try number one: no success. I turned the key again, nothing. I silenced the engine, sat for a bit, and tried again. This process continued for an hour or so until we gave up.

When my dad said it was time to go inside, I practically ran everybody over, but Austin didn't follow. He walked in the opposite direction. Though I thought it was odd he was going to the basketball court to practice, I shrugged it off and went inside to shower off the manure and dirt that had collected in my hair. When I finished, Austin was waiting patiently (for once) to claim the shower for himself. His face was dirty, his brown hair lightly dusted with manure and sagebrush.

When Austin decided that day that he would take one of his infamous half-hour showers, our parents told us they were going to church without us since we weren't ready. When I was young, I attended Mass every Sunday. Confession: I rarely listened or paid attention. Of course I believed in God, but I never fully understood the concept of faith. I remember falling asleep during Mass and the priest embarrassed me in front of everyone by telling me to wake up.

I had no idea then that, when I got older, I would need an entirely different wakeup call. Church was just me going through the motions and my parents telling me to be quiet. Looking back now, I wish I had laid a better foundation for myself.

That day was the first time, outside of illness, that our parents decided to leave us at home. They told me that, while they were gone, we were to clean the kitchen. I remember thinking, "I thought all our chores were finished. I'm going to wait until Austin is out here to help, because it's not fair to do this by myself." I was stubborn and had a strong sense of fair and unfair. I also knew how to use words to push everyone's buttons. Strangely, though, Austin's buttons weren't easy to push that day. When we were younger and lived in Douglas in our ranch home, Austin had a treehouse, and I pushed his buttons by writing my name all over the inside with permanent marker. He retaliated by locking me in my playhouse. After three hours, I retaliated by breaking the windows open. But years later, on that day in November of 2008, my parents unintentionally pushed his buttons when they told him our seventeen-year-old cousin, Chad, wanted to go bunny bashing with him. Austin curtly told them he didn't want to go. I should pause here and explain about bunny bashing. It's something of a game you play when surrounded by acres of fields. The object is to stun a rabbit with a club or a bat. Yes, for some it may sound horrifying, but think of it this way: rabbits eat our crops, spoiling it for our cattle and harvesting and plowing. Austin declined to join Chad. I don't know if it was because of the game itself, or perhaps he just wasn't interested that day.

While we were cleaning the kitchen, my brother received a text message from a girl he had met at camp. I told him he should read it, but he said he didn't want to. Austin was good looking, and he knew it.

Girls always wanted to go places with him and talk to him. I remember when I was in first grade, Austin had a girlfriend, even though he was only in the third grade. Her name was Ally. She lived down the street, and she often walked to our house to see him. For her birthday, Austin decided to give Ally my clothes, probably because I had quite a few due to my mother and grandmother being chronic shoppers. Our mother, of course, made sure I got them back. In the beginning, Ally's crush was cute, but her visits to our home became excessive. It got to the point that when she appeared on our doorstep, my parents often told her Austin wasn't home.

While we were cleaning the kitchen, Austin's words to me mostly consisted of things like: "Let's get this done with", "Bridget, you're going too slow", and "When we are done, I get Mom and Dad's room to watch TV." All I could think was, "I'm hurrying and do what you want." I knew he was tired, so I was tolerant and tried to be pleasant. Regardless of everything we did that day, I was not tired. After we cleaned the kitchen, it looked immaculate—well, by our standards. My mom took great pride in her kitchen and, in our opinion, she was one step away from being a gourmet chef. Even though she had a major in Spanish and French, she had quit her job as a teacher to become a full-time mom. I was truly blessed to have her. We always came home from our sports practices tired, hungry, and irritable, but as soon as we smelled her cooking, we ached for dinnertime. Often, I would delay my homework to help her cook so I could taste the dinner beforehand. It always amazed me how she could wake up at the crack of dawn, cook breakfast, drive us to school, do laundry, clean the house, attend all our games, and support us in our studies until we were fluent in our subjects.

I followed my brother to our parents' room. Before he could slam the door in my face, I managed to say, "If you need me, I'll be in my room." All he said was "Okay." He shut the door, and I failed to notice the clicking of the door's lock. This was the last time I would speak to Austin. This was the last time I would see him alive. If only I had known.

I am only sixteen years old as I write this, and over three years have passed since this day, but it seems to me that we often don't stop to savor the moment. We take for granted important moments in our lives, the ones God has planned for us for a reason.

Around 5:00 p.m., I answered a phone call from our cousin who asked to talk to Austin in the hope he could convince him to join him in his bunny bashing adventure. Wearing pajamas and my usual mismatched socks, my hair soaking wet, I walked from my room to our parents' room. I turned the knob and discovered it was locked. It occurred to me that Austin was doing something he didn't want me to know about. It also occurred to me that I might catch him in the act.

I went out onto our back patio that had the best view facing south where all the fields lined up alongside each other. On the left side of the patio was the glass sliding door of our parents' room. The seconds that followed changed my life—all of our lives—forever.

There was that cold water. It swept over my toes, clawed its way up my arms, wrapped its icy fingers around my neck. Numb. When it reached my brain, it felt as if I were spinning. What I saw in front of me wasn't believable. And yet, through that sliding glass door, I saw Austin and red—so much red that the color was unfamiliar. I couldn't comprehend the meaning. Then I saw something else that was just as foreign. A gun. I tried to put the pieces together, but all of their ends were different. Had my brother really shot himself, or was this an accident?

I screamed Austin's name and the phone flew out of my hand. Another possibility occurred to me—that someone was at our house and had done this! I understand that most people, when hit with tragedy, have no sense of perception and reality, but I had too much. I looked around, checking to see if anything else was off. My stomach twisted so violently that I almost lost consciousness. I thought I might be dreaming and tried to convince myself this wasn't real. I grabbed my phone off the porch and speed-dialed my best friend.

The dial tone seemed to mock me, but finally, I heard her voice. "Hey Bridget!" My cousin, Sandy, who at the time was forty-five minutes away in Carson City, was the sister I never had and a role model. We weren't very close until I entered middle school and we played sports together. I always tried to be just like her because she was the toughest girl I had ever met.

I screamed her name.

"What's going on Bridget?" she demanded. All I could manage to do was trip over my words until I screamed Austin's name and spat out, "He shot himself." I fell to the porch and it felt as if my upper body was moving in a circular direction, then my whole body was moving with it, much like the rides at the rodeo I had enjoyed when I was younger. You would spin so hard and fast, that you had no control of yourself. I cannot remember how Sandy responded, but I hung up knowing she would do the right thing since her dad was the sheriff of our county.

Shakily, I dialed "9-1-1". Dispatch answered and I said, "My brother shot himself." Somehow, I knew this was a fact and that no one else had done it. The woman asked a few simple questions that set off my temper. I hung up on her. A few minutes later, while

I lay on the porch crying out Austin's name and hoping he would wake up, dispatch called again and told me that help was on the way. I was scared—scared of the rest of my life, the night to come, and the moment I would see my parents. I squeezed my eyes closed, then quickly opened them. I thought of Austin with God and imagined him looking down on me and realizing what he had done. But was God really there?

Crouching outside the glass doors, I looked at Austin who lay on carpet that should have been white. Instead, it was my brother's face that was white, almost transparent. The way his body lay looked so uncomfortable and unnatural. I wish that wasn't the last image I had of Austin, but I had no choice in the matter. And I know it will stay with me for a lifetime.

For what seemed hours, I played the "if" game: if only I could do something, if only I could go back ten minutes, if only I had some control.

The strength required to lift my body from the cold ground was immense. In my unmatched socks, I walked to the nearest neighbor's house. These elderly neighbors were the type of people who are organized to the pin and they had hearts of gold. They had two small lap dogs and chickens in their yard.

I knocked on the door and when it creaked open, I could only imagine what I looked like. Their reaction to the sight of me is another memory that has made itself at home in my thoughts. Once again, I struggled for words until I was able to spit them out. The lady took me into her house, wrapped a towel around my wet hair, and put a jacket on me. I somehow managed to tell her I had phoned 9-1-1 and the police were on their way. She helped me into her car and sped toward my church where my parents were.

As I sat beside my neighbor, I was comforted in knowing I wasn't alone anymore. The feeling impacted me and I realized that humans need each other. The wave of comfort subsided and urgency took its place. "I have to be with my parents," I said. "I have to tell them."

When we reached the church, I got out of the car. Alone again, I opened the stained glass doors and, for the first time, disregarded their beauty. To this day, I can still see the congregation vividly. People knelt with their backs to me, all heads were bowed, including those of the priests—until they heard the patter of my socks over the carpet. As I passed each pew, heads came up one by one. I saw some of my friends and was consoled by their presence.

When I reached my parents, their faces reflected confusion, but they knew something terrible must have happened to bring me to church and rose from their pew and exited with me.

Only three words were needed, and yet they were so hard to speak—"Austin shot himself." Growing up on a ranch, I had been exposed to death, so I was pretty certain my brother was dead. However, what I had seen through the glass doors was so unbearable I couldn't yet embrace it. Minutes moved like seconds as we drove to our home. I remember my mom grabbing my hand in the car and praying everything would be fine and we would have our smiling boy back.

On our front lawn, we were met by my uncle who was Sandy and Chad's dad, another officer, and Chad who was a firefighter. Chad and my uncle had knocked down the door to get to Austin. My mom was sheer white, though I suppose all of us were. She asked the other police officer about Austin's condition. His words still haunt me: "I am sorry, but he is deceased." Holding onto each other, my mother and I collapsed on the grass.

LOOKING BACK...

I didn't know how to move forward in life. For many tweens, it seems the biggest worry is getting homework done, perhaps even what to do during recess. The worry on my horizon was how to move on with my life and how my parents and family would be affected. The transition in my life was drastic and instant. I was scared of what lay ahead.

Kids from my school sent me text messages with pictures of my brother and texts that read: "RIP Austin Jon Park." I received several messages each day, and I replied back, asking the senders to stop sending the messages. I got so fed up with the messages and phone calls that my parents and I blocked people on my phone so they couldn't contact me. I eventually learned that kids grieve differently, but I never liked the way they grieved over my brother. They acted as if they knew him better than I did.

Most of my peers weren't sensitive to my feelings, which often upset me. One girl in particular said, over and over again, "He was like a brother to me" and "He was like my best friend." Though I no longer received phone messages, when people began posting on social networking sites, I became angrier. It was a constant reminder that my brother was gone.

mourning

There are times that life passes you by as if you're in a car on a highway staring past all objects and focusing on absolutely nothing. In that moment on the front lawn with my mom and the police officer, everything went blurry as I fell to the ground. I was so overwhelmed, confused, and distraught that my balance failed me. While I lay there, I had another mental breakdown. "Is he really dead? Is this real? What do I do now? Why did this happen to me?" These questions and more stormed my mind.

Some time later, Chad helped me up and braced me against his body. We walked to his truck so he could take me to his house where I could be with Sandy. The ride was silent. I didn't know where my parents were, but later I heard that the priest who had been conducting the Mass I interrupted, dismissed the congregation early so he could come to my house to console my parents. My brain rewound and replayed the events that had taken place in the past hour.

Chad escorted me to Sandy's room and I laid face down on her bed to wait for her. I inhaled and exhaled deeply in an attempt to push out my fear and anguish. Occasionally, Chad came into the room and offered me food or water, but I couldn't think straight let alone eat or drink.

I wondered where my parents were and what the people in church had thought when I walked in. I knew that, because of my new situation and that I lived in a small town, people would talk about me and my family. Worst of all, they would talk about Austin. Maybe some would honor him or remember him with love, and maybe others would call him mentally ill. Anger grew in me, and I immediately directed it at Austin. I didn't blame God for taking him, because I knew Austin was the one who had made the decision. But I did blame God for not saving him or giving him a second chance at life.

Sandy arrived home and joined me. As we lay on the bed side by side, her mom tried to comfort me with an early birthday present. It was thirteen days before my thirteenth birthday, and she had bought me plush sheep slippers. I thanked her for the gift, went into the bathroom, and splashed water on my face.

I don't know how I remember so many details of what happened that night. I tried to block out all thoughts of Austin and what had happened. Despite the shock and pain I felt, I did not yet know I was grieving. That night, Sandy and I were taken to my grandparents' home by a family friend and I immediately went to bed. As I lay next to Sandy who was sleeping, my mind overflowed with thoughts and memories. Even though it was only hours since the event, it seemed like days. I listened to the moans and cries of my parents who were upstairs. It was a sound I would never want anyone to hear. I turned on the television to try to drown it out and, at some point, my uncle gave me sleeping pills to help me sleep. Unfortunately, the pills failed me. I still feel pain in my heart when I remember the cries exerted by my parents.

Prior to Austin's death, my uncle and dad hadn't been very close, but in spite of the pain caused by my parents' cries, a part of me was overjoyed by the compassion my uncle was showing my father.

Though I was blessed to have grandparents who would open their house up to my family and who would take care of us no matter what, that night the house felt like a train wreck. People constantly came in and out, either to visit or deliver meals. I tried to shove every feeling under the rug. I didn't want to feel the pain. I didn't want to grieve. I didn't want to show any signs of weakness. I became a brick wall. Looking back, I deeply regret that I shut down, because I believe it caused me to suppress memories of Austin that are still missing to this day.

Days later, preparations for the funeral were underway. Sandy and I moved between her house and my grandparents' house on a daily basis. I didn't eat a lot and I often laid in bed with the warmth of Sandy's body to console me. I was never alone. I had friends who came to see me and bring gifts of food and comfort. I was blessed to have those people there to support me. Members of our community took over the care of our home and set up our Christmas tree in our living room. We were surrounded by people who loved us.

I despised anyone who spoke of my brother as if they were closer to him than I was or believed they knew what had happened. Rumors were spreading like wildfire. In a larger town, twenty minutes away, some people were saying that Austin and I got in a fight and I was the one who pulled the trigger. Worse, this rumor originated with a family friend who was thriving on having the "inside scoop." My thoughts were "Screw you. I hate all of you. My life is hell and you're messing it up more. You don't deserve my friendship."

Soon, Sandy was the only friend in whom I felt I could trust and confide. When others visited me, I mentally turned off. If they asked a question, I gave the vaguest answer possible. Inside, I was raging: "How dare they ask me how I'm doing when they think they know everything that happened?" I put more energy into hatred than I did in remembering my brother. My anger made me go in continuous circles, and I didn't try to hide it. I wanted people to know they didn't know Austin like I had. Every moment after his death I was just "there." I was living but not alive.

Of all the visitors, I was most affected by my brother's friend, Devin. He was two years older than Austin, but they were good friends and had a lot in common. Though I didn't know Devin previous to Austin's death, he is family to me now. I felt he was worthy to be one of Austin's friends. He visited me and Sandy at her house. All he brought was humor, but it was the greatest gift. It allowed me to let go of some of the anger and resentment, and it felt like a weight was being lifted off my shoulders. But I didn't know that this was only temporary.

I dreaded the funeral, rosary, and school memorial. I wanted to stay with my family and not reach out to others. I wanted to remain in my personal bubble and comfort zone. I was being self-ish. I now realize that I was so miserable that I didn't honor my brother and support my family as I should have. But at the same time, being surrounded by my family helped me heal and begin to feel my way back to a semblance of happiness. My extended family had never been close, and it's a shame that it took this tragedy to pull us together.

CLIPPINGS

"A rosary will be said 7 p.m. today at St. John's Catholic Church in Smith for seventh-generation Nevadan Austin Jon Park, 14, who died Nov. 29, 2008, at his home in Smith Valley. A community vigil will follow the service 8 p.m. at the Smith Valley High School Gymnasium.

A funeral is 10 a.m. Thursday at St. Gall Catholic Church in Gardnerville, with burial immediately following at Mottsville Cemetery. A reception will follow in the pastoral center at St. Gall Catholic Church.

Austin was born Feb. 22, 1994, to a pioneer Carson Valley family. An accomplished student at Smith Valley High School, family members said he excelled in everything he did, and looked forward to each new endeavor that life brought his way. From his role in the Future Farmers of America, to playing halfback and linebacker with the Smith Valley Bulldogs, Austin simply had a good time being a boy. He also played junior varsity basketball and was looking forward to the upcoming season and his favorite sport, track and field.

Austin enjoyed spending time with his friends and family. His sister, Bridget, could always count on him for anything and to his parents, Joe and Jen Park, he was their utmost joy. From childhood friends to his adult peers, Austin had a sincerity and friendliness that was infectious to all those who had the honor of being part of a life that was taken all too soon. He is survived by his parents, Joe and Jen Park; sister Bridget Park; grandparents Bob and Barbara Park, grandmother Susan Whittaker, grandparents Katherine and James Dowd, great-grandmother Norma Gomes and other loving family members."

Never would I have guessed I would be reading my brother's obituary before the age of thirteen. In my grandparent's living room on their black leather couch, I lay silent, re-reading the words in front of me. I was more mentally stable once I got out of the state of shock, but now I had another obstacle: going to Austin's services and seeing unwanted people. Because of the rumors, I wanted my brother's death to be my secret. That was, of course, impossible. I began to have a weird feeling that Austin was a fictional character I had created in my mind. However, I knew somewhere deep inside my story was proof that I really did have a brother.

THE ROSARY

At my grandparents' home, I observed the people around me as if I was passing by and not there to stay. I greeted my grandparents on my mother's side and, for the first time, saw tears in their eyes. I felt that, eventually, I would be able to deal with my own pain, but it broke me to see others grieve. Deep pain pierced my soul. It's mind blowing that one person can have such an impact on other people's lives.

On December 3, 2008, I considered my reflection in the mirror for the first time in a long time. My face was pale and there seemed no evidence that emotion had ever been comfortable on my face. My blonde hair was carefully styled, yet my eyes seemed woven with confusion, nervousness, and despair. My mom stood to my right, staring at her own reflection. I saw the bags under her eyes that accentuated her tired, expressionless face. Sandy was to my left. After putting her orange rosary around her neck, she handed mine to me. I wondered how I was supposed to pray a rosary for someone who was taken from me so soon and cruelly. My mind paced slowly from one thought to the next and I could feel my heart stoop lower and lower in my motionless body. But then I remembered something. I remembered my mother telling Austin and me when we were younger that her brother, Matthew, had died when he was 17 and she was 15. She was raised by her mother after her father left them when she was young. I never wanted to ask how Matthew had died, but looking at my mom's eyes in the mirror, I knew it was the same way Austin had died.

When we arrived at the church, I was dressed in black dress pants and a black blouse. The day before the rosary, my dear Aunt Carrie had taken me shopping since I didn't have clothes besides the pajamas I had been wearing that day. She was so kind. I admire her to this day for what she did for me. The only color I wore besides black was the pink of my beaded rosary that I had received as a gift from a family friend.

We entered the church, and I remembered that the last time I was there, I had been searching for my parents. I relived it all. This time, however, I was appropriately dressed and wasn't as hysterical—at least, not on the outside. Inside, I felt out of place in my life.

My family was already seated in the front row. I bowed before the Lord to honor his presence, knelt on the floor, and clutched my rosary tight. When I stood, I lifted my head and looked around the church. All the seats were taken and people were lined up outside the church waiting to go into the basement to make more room. My brother was honored that night.

Though I knew there would be people there I didn't like, I also knew deep down that there were more good people than bad. When I turned my face forward again, I caught sight of a large, metallic blue box and wondered what it was. My dad walked up to the altar. He put his head on the box and cried while my uncle stroked his back and supported his dead weight on the box. The box was foreign to me, but not for long.

"Is Austin really in there? Can I feel his presence through the box? Or is his spirit locked in there forever?" My heart pounded with the hope I would be able to feel some sort of emotion sent from Austin's spirit.

As the rosary was being led aloud, I bowed my head and stared at my rosary. It represented my new, changed life and whenever I saw it, I felt hope that someday, something good would come out of this tragedy. I vowed that, from that day forward, I would never remove the rosary. But my tears represented the hurt and pain deep inside that could finally be released openly.

At the end of the rosary, everyone gathered around the altar to comfort one another. I observed everyone and their body language. Some looked distressed, others uncomfortable. I saw my other uncle for the first time in a few years. I was surprised he had come. My aunt and uncle had been divorced for a few years and it was good to see him interact with me and our family. I approached the blue box and touched it. With my fingers, I lightly traced the metal lining and rejected the absent feeling of Austin. Even though the casket was closed, I imagined Austin inside. I wanted him to spring out of the box and give us a big, old smile and say he was back forever. But I needed to get it through my head that would never happen.

THE VIGIL

Down the road from our church, another challenge awaited me: the high school vigil. I knew I would see my friends, as well as people I preferred not to see. I braced myself for the worst and put on a façade that said I was untouchable. As I walked into the gym, my arm linked with Sandy's, I saw familiar faces and those of friends and their parents. Their expressions were sorrowful and full of pity. I felt their love, compassion, and sincerity radiating from their hearts into mine. Step by step, more faces appeared: boys in football jerseys, people in black, people hiding their faces.

I bowed my head to avoid eye contact. I felt shame, as if I were to blame. Maybe I felt like people actually believed the terrible rumors that I had pulled the trigger. Again, we were seated in the front row. One person after another walked up to the podium and spoke words of sympathy to my family. The football team spoke of Austin and their good memories of him.

Family friends told stories of Austin and some demonstrated his smile when he would laugh. After each person finished sharing, they showed more sympathy for my family by hugging and embracing each of us.

Candle lighting followed the memories. Everyone was given a candle to light for Austin. I looked around the gym. One side of the bleachers were full. The other side was covered with cards and posters for my family including the whole gym floor. In front of everyone was Austin's desk from one of his classes, along with his football jersey (#22), and school picture that had been enlarged. The lights went out, but then hundreds of flickering lights were illuminated. I saw a camera flash at me, and I felt like a celebrity for the wrong reason. Again, another flash, then another.

The day of the funeral, I woke up next to Sandy. I got out of bed and trudged to the bathroom where I splashed water on my face. This time, I saw a girl who was broken on the inside but who looked pulled together on the outside. I had managed to erect a façade that no one could see through. Whenever memories of that terrible night visited me, I simply told myself "That didn't happen."

In the kitchen, my whole family looked distraught and in a panic. My mom and dad were overseeing the funeral arrangements by themselves. I admired the incredible strength required for them to do so. My grandmother prepared me a wonderful breakfast of eggs and bacon, but I could only stare at it. On the table next to my breakfast was the local newspaper, The Record Courier. My picture was on the front page, my head bowed as I looked dead into the candle that lit up my face. In the background were the tiny lights of candles held by those in attendance. Below the picture, highlights of the vigil and rosary were listed:

"A signed football and Austin Jon Park's Smith Valley Bulldogs jersey became the symbols for a vigil held by students in Smith on Wednesday night.

Four of Austin's teammates hugged members of his family after talking about the 14-year-old student, who died Saturday at his home.

More than 250 people packed the multipurpose room at Smith Valley School to say farewell to Austin, a member of a Carson Valley pioneer family.

In the vigil organized by his classmates, students hugged and comforted one another.

Student Kelly Smith offered the family her condolences from her classmates.

"This is not just from me," she said. "It is to and from all of us. Austin was always the life of the party. He was always interested in making a thing cooler. We are all Bulldogs, just as Austin would have wanted us to be."

Austin attended the rural Smith Valley School for a year and a half, according to Principal. The school has 221 students kindergarten through 12th grade. About 121 of them are considered high school students. She said she expected the vast majority of them to attend services in Gardnerville held Thursday.

Teammate running back Devin Caughfeild told students that at the game against rival Coleville, even though the Bulldogs were 30 points down, when Austin made a touchdown he still made a fist pump.

GROWING YOUNG

Wide receiver Anthony Gomez called Austin an amazing person. "If there's a football team in Heaven, then Austin is on it," he said.

Megan Anderson said Austin joined the FFA Dairy Team when it went to nationals in October. She described part of the initiation as eating White Castle burgers. After some goading, Austin finally partook, only to have them come back up. "Even then, he came back with a big smile," she said. "I'll always, always remember that."

Students prepared a 15-minute slideshow about Austin and his activities. Between photos, they'd written messages to Austin and his family.

"I will never forget your smiling face," wrote Natalie Lind.

"I will miss you forever," said Brett Jacobs.

At the beginning of the service, Student Body President Jullianne Lauffer told family members how much they would miss Austin. "He was always willing to help someone in need," she said.

After the vigil, mourners lit candles in Austin's memory.

A website has been set up for Austin at www.austin-jonpark.last-memories.com, so that people may leave their condolences.

As of Thursday, the site had attracted more than 90 posts.

A former Carson Valley resident, Austin was born Feb. 22, 1994, in Carson City.

In addition to Smith Valley football, Austin played for Douglas Tiger Pop Warner football, and was an award-winning Carson Valley Middle School wrestler. A good student, Austin won $100 at the Douglas County Spelling Bee as a participant from Minden Elementary School in February 2006.

He is survived by his parents, Joe and Jen Park; sister Bridget Park; grandparents Bob and Barbara Park, Grandmother Suzan Whittaker, grandparents Katherine and James Dowd, great-grandmother Norma Gomes and other family members."

Austin playing football his freshman year of high school.

THE FUNERAL

600 faces, some familiar, some not so familiar. Sandy and I wore black dresses. I hadn't made much of an effort to look presentable since there seemed no reason to look good on such an occasion. I knew we had some part to play in the funeral, but I didn't care much about it. My attitude was, "Let's get this done with."

Through observation, I was learning that all humans grieve differently. My mother was well put together in front of me, but now I know that behind the door of her emotions was a vulnerable woman. In contrast, my dad was emotional and helpless. He expressed grief with every look on his face. As he had always been a strong man who told me not to cry when I was younger, it was odd to see him in this state. He had been taught as a young child in the Catholic Church that if you committed suicide, you went to Hell. He was having a hard time believing that my brother would go to Heaven. As for me, I had no doubt that Heaven was Austin's destination.

I managed to stay strong in front of my parents, so I could comfort them. Whether I was alone or in public, I wore a mask. "Death happens all the time, right?" I reasoned. Sooner or later, it happens to everyone, and I knew I shouldn't be shocked. I told myself to snap out of it since I didn't want to look weak or helpless. I wanted to be strong for everyone—at least, everyone who was close to me.

For the third time that week, I walked down the aisle of a church before a large crowd of people, and I realized how tired I was of the process—head down, eyes focused on the floor, Sandy at my side. My family and I proceeded through the church behind the blue box that I was beginning to call by its real name—casket. Seeing everyone there, the hundreds of people who loved my family and me, made me incredibly emotional. My mask wasn't thick enough to hold everything inside. Each step forward seemed to represent progression in my life. Though the rosary and vigil had been easier than expected, the funeral was harder than I would ever have imagined. I was in another state of mind. I felt like I had to act proper and portray myself as a girl who was strong enough to comfort others around me. I tried, but I was so weak and vulnerable that I failed to be that girl. Disappointed in myself, I kissed Austin's casket, as if it was goodbye, and took my seat.

The priest who presided over the funeral was my favorite. I had grown up listening to him. At Christmas, he gave all the young children stuffed animals and I enjoyed church. But this time, there was no joy to be found at church or in seeing him. The Mass went on as normal with a homily about Heaven and God's forgiveness of all sins. More people shared memories of my brother. My mom's best friend, Jackie, spoke of the times she had babysat Austin. "He was so picky!" she exclaimed. "He would only eat hotdogs and apple-flavored Nutrigrain bars." Everyone seemed to enjoy that story as much as I did. When I went forward to receive Communion, I felt as if burdens were upon me. I didn't even consider prayer, because it had failed me Saturday night on the way to my house when my mother and I had joined hands and prayed. My life had been perfect until this tragedy. Why pray when it had failed me at the time I most needed it?

At the end of the service, another picture slideshow closed the service. There were pictures of Austin and me that I had never seen. They brought me so much unexpected joy that I thought I would burst with happiness. I suppose it hadn't really hit me that he was gone forever. His death seemed only a memory that wasn't planted in my brain and I didn't plan to plant it. I was determined to push it farther back until it was so distant it would seem more like an idea or a figment of my imagination. I didn't quite understand it then, but I was trying to avoid grief and pain.

*Austin holding me a few
days after I was born.*

My brother, 6, and me, 4.

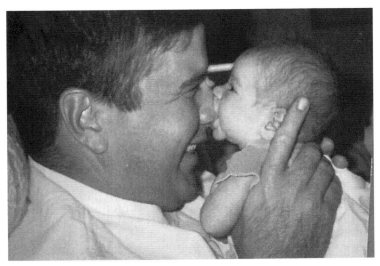

My dad and baby Austin.

These pictures are my favorite pictures of Austin that I keep near at all times. They show how happy we were and are a reflection of the good times we shared over the years. Though I felt like I should not totally forget about Austin, I believed I shouldn't grieve and that it was best if I simply acted happy. It seemed like a good plan.

At the cemetery Austin was placed in our family plot. It was raining which added to the feeling of distress. I felt as if I were in a movie and I sensed that I was missing something or had to do something. I took off my high heels to avoid blisters and sinking into the mud. Though I was surrounded by many people, I felt alone as I stared deeply into the hole in the ground before me. The rain dripped down the strands of hair that hung over my face. I felt peace and embraced it, but it didn't last long. My dad's mother came and sat next to me. She and I weren't really close since she and my grandpa had divorced long before I was born and she had moved out of the area. My eyes were still fixed on the hole when she suddenly said, "Bridget, I love you." She hugged me. I was amazed that a gesture so many of us take for granted could be so magical in a moment like that. I often received hugs from my family and friends, but I didn't think much of them. That hug on that day was special.

The pallbearers moved in a pack in their black suits, their faces solemn. The closer they got, the more their synchronized steps made reality of the moment. People followed behind, their umbrellas opened to ward off the rain. I didn't mind the rain. The cold made me feel alive; the only feeling that seemed normal. Each drop refreshed my senses, and I found myself longing to fly above everyone and be with Austin and watch those below us.

Some of my friends from when I was younger attended the funeral. When our eyes met, they quickly looked away. I thought how peculiar it was that my best friend from age 5 to 8 acted as though I was a stranger on the street. Memories we had made together raced through my mind—sleepovers, movie nights, days at the beach. Though I know not all relationships are weakened when friends part and time stretches between them, that is how it felt for me that day. It was as if someone else had lived that first half of my life. I put my feet in the mud. The slush oozed between my toes, the cold invigorated my skin, and I felt mystical inside. The casket drew nearer, and the faces of those in black suits became more defined. They were members of Austin's football team. I met each of their gazes in an attempt to express my gratitude.

The priest said words that made me drift into another world. I stared mindlessly at the fields of sagebrush bordering the cemetery. The sagebrush mesmorized me as if it would know me forever. For me, it felt as if the gray, dusty weed represented my new life. I heard mumbling and snapped back to reality to find the priest asking me if I wanted to put anything with Austin before he was buried. I stood, shoved my muddy feet into my high heels, and circled the casket.

Staring blankly, I put a football in the casket, the same football that Austin and our father had used to play catch.

During the slideshow at church, there had been a picture of the two of them on our back lawn playing football. In it, Austin was lunging forward. Our dad gripped the football against his side and was slightly turned as if to dodge Austin. Dad loved football and especially enjoying playing with my brother. When Austin was ten years old, he didn't want to play football. He enjoyed Taekwondo. Though he was almost a black belt, he decided he wanted to do something new, so my dad bribed Austin and his friend to try football. By the end of the first week, Austin adored the sport. Unfortunately, his friend didn't feel the same. During my brother's second year of playing football, our dad coached his team and the sport strengthened their bond.

When I had placed the football in the casket, I imagined that my dad knew those sunny days on the back lawn were over. The football wasn't a symbol of the sport itself, but of the common interest they had treasured.

Following the burial, we returned to church where a reception was held in the multipurpose room. Comfort food, provided by our family-owned golf course, was served. Sandy and my aunts, Mary and Teresa, sat with me in a back corner where we hid from anyone who might want to talk to us. I was overwhelmed by all the people who wanted to see me and my family. Over and over again, I heard "Sorry," but it didn't really help. "Why apologize for something out of your control?" I thought. I felt bad for leaving my parents with all the people and their condolences, but there is only so much one person can handle.

Sandy had a bag of rubber bracelets that had been made for Austin. They were orange, his favorite color, and were engraved with: "In Loving Memory of Austin Jon Park." I snatched a handful of them to use as replacements.

"These are only for people who deserve them," I told Sandy. "Keep them under the table so no one can take them." I had a grudge against all the girls who had treated my brother wrong. Since we attended a small school, some of these girls had been my friends. As I sat there staring at the bracelets, I remembered when my brother was in eighth grade and dated a girl named Sheri. She was nice, at least when she was around Austin. When she was around me, I wasn't her boyfriend's little sister. I was the girl she could easily harass. Thankfully, their "love" lasted only a short while. When they broke up, Austin started crushing on Sheri's friend. She led him on and, when Austin asked her to be his girlfriend, she turned him down and proudly admitted she had led him on to avenge Sheri. Those two girls and others didn't deserve a bracelet, even though I knew they would get their hands on one.

When we left the sanctuary of the corner and returned to our table, we saw two girls from our school who had handfuls of the bracelets. One of them had stood up Austin at homecoming, another called him and twenty other guys her "best friend." Anger rose in me so fast that my head pounded. Austin would not be honored with those girls wearing his bracelet.

You have to understand that I believed I was the only girl in my brother's life. Those girls didn't deserve him. I was the one who looked up to him and loved him with all my heart and soul. Siblings fight, especially teens, but I never doubted the strength of our relationship.

When I finally arrived home, I stripped off my clothing, minus my rosary. Along with the mud, I tried to wash off my anger, hatred, and confusion. I felt pure. I felt peace. I felt whole again. But when I turned off the faucet, the comforting warmth fled. I took one step out of the shower, opened the bedroom door, and saw that Sandy lay silently on the bed. Her shoulders heaved. Peace in temporary happiness, I learned.

Two weeks later, a Catholic Youth minister from Carson City came to Smith Valley to form a support group. We met in the church's basement and there were about 30 people crammed into the room. A man with a strong Louisianan accent introduced himself as Rick and gave us a mini biography. He told the story about his cousin, Amy, and how she had died. He told us that, weeks later, he was issued a new license plate. To his surprise, the three numbers on it were followed by the letters A-M-Y. Rick said the plate was a sign that his cousin was okay in Heaven. He told us we needed to vent because a death affects a lot of people in many ways and, therefore, he was going to partner us with someone in the room. Once, every week, we would tell the group how we were doing. Just my luck, I was partnered with Rick, the overzealous youth minister.

My priest from my church reading some of the cards
Austin's friends and classmates made for his vigil at school.
Photo Credits to The Record Courier Newspaper.

LOOKING BACK...

Returning to school was awkward and terrifying. I didn't know what people were going to do or say. I felt like I had to pretend to be someone I wasn't. I was afraid to laugh or crack a smile for fear some might think I didn't miss or love Austin.

I set myself apart from the world, because I felt like I was dreaming and that this life wasn't mine at all. I spent most lunch breaks in the bathroom or office. I hid from what I was afraid of: people. No one understood me, which is now understandable. It felt as if no one tried to relate.

I found comfort in listening to and writing music. I didn't like the idea of writing in a journal, so I wrote songs and ballads. In two years, I filled up two journals with songs. I would never perform them, just reflect on them. I had always had a passion for singing, but I didn't take myself too seriously. After I filled up both journals, I destroyed them. It was a way to move on from my pain and sometimes even my joy. I believed I needed to start from scratch in every chapter in my life. I felt relief pour out of me when I destroyed them. It meant starting over and, most importantly, forgetting.

There were songs that made me think of Austin...that made me miss him...that made me want to cry:

Because of You by Kelly Clarkson—reflected how angry I was with God
Sissy's Song by Alan Jackson—a message of how good Heaven is and that there is no end to a relationship
Heaven by DJ Sammy—made me feel like Austin was with me again and there was hope for our family
I'll Be Missing You by Puff Daddy—played at memorial
Temporary Home by Carrie Underwood—made me realize that death is life, there is always Heaven, and death is not the end

Music helped me express how I felt. It allowed me to spill out my feelings and forced my locked up emotions to override my brain and let my heart take over.

I received many gifts that first month following Austin's death. Many of them were journals. Unfortunately, writing never really helped me. It made me think too much about how I felt, and I struggled over what to write. I substituted coloring book pictures for writing since it was a relatively mindless activity. All you had to do was stay in the lines and your mind could wander. Following Austin's death, I had a lot of missing schoolwork, and one teacher allowed me to color to make up for the work, but only if I gave her my pictures and wrote on them that she was my favorite teacher. Looking back, I don't believe this was handled correctly, but I know she was well intentioned.

I was influenced to make all sorts of "art." I never liked to call it art because I wasn't artistic. If I was having a bad night, I would pull out a piece of paper and make something like this:

I wrote down the emotions I felt in a style that reflected each emotion.

A close family friend gave me a light up butterfly that, when I plugged it in at night, changed its color every few minutes. I think of my brother now as a butterfly. Every spring time when I see one, especially an orange monarch, I know it's Austin or his soul saying "hi" to me. It was my most prized possession, for it brought me comfort and hope knowing that butterflies are beautiful and happy, like Austin in Heaven.

clueless

Sandy returned to her home and school, and for two weeks we lived at my grandparents' second home in Yerington, a twenty-minute drive from my school. I stayed in my favorite room, which was known as the Lavender Room because everything in it was that color. Every morning when I woke up, the sun shined on the room perfectly turning it iridescent.

Though we weren't close to moving back into our country home, preparations were being made. Since the carpet in my parents' bedroom would be forever stained red, a reminder that none of us could live with, new carpet was ordered for the whole house and represented something of a clean start.

We were now in the month of December. Though my thirteenth birthday was only a week away, I had no intention of indulging in any sort of celebration.

The next hurdle I faced was going back to school. My mom told me that in one week I would have to return. I was mortified at the thought of being separated from my family and being placed in awkward situations. "Mom, people will treat me differently," I argued. "They'll try to act like they're my friends, and I don't want their pity."

"Bridget," she said, "do it to get it over with. People will pity you. Maybe they feel they owe you some compassion, but rightly so. Just accept it knowing you don't have to be best friends with them." To help me and my peers adjust, my mom told me our family had offered to pay for grief counselors to come to school and counsel the students and staff.

On the day I returned to school, the sun shone into the Lavender Room and made my eyes flutter open. The dreaded day had arrived.

What do I wear?

Black. And my rosary, of course.

Do I go early?

No, show up late to avoid socializing.

Okay, Bridget, you can make it through the day. Rush to each class. Eat lunch in the counselor's office.

My mind blabbered on, but I thought the plan was ingenious. On top of being self-conscious about my looks, I now had the stress of social outbursts I was certain would come my way. Life as a soon-to-be-teenager was hard enough. "God, when will I ever get a break?" Praying wasn't high on my list of priorities, but getting the day over with was.

My first period class was typing. Daily, the teacher tried to convince us that typing fast was a necessity in middle school. I had always dreaded that class, but on my first day back to school, I was anxious. All fifteen of us in the 7th grade had our classes together. When

I walked into the classroom five minutes late, all eyes that should have been fixed on computer screens turned to me and stared.

My friend broke the silence. "Bridget!" She ran to me and hugged me tight. "We all missed you." It sounded more like concern than a statement, as if she hadn't received the response she was hoping for.

I didn't believe I should be happy or fake being happy to be back at school or to see any of these people. I knew she loved me as a friend, but there was just too much pity behind her greeting. I don't think I thought of myself as a victim of suicide, but neither did I consider myself a survivor. After all, a survivor goes on suicide walks and talks joyously of lost loved ones. My reasoning was far from cerebral. My judgment was far from typical. But since my life had changed, I knew I had to adapt. I believed I had to change my thoughts, actions, clothes, and everything about me to adjust to my new life of grief and gloom. Happiness no longer seemed an option, so I chose not to be happy.

I sat down in my seat next to a boy with eyes that were magnified by thick-rimmed glasses.

"Hey Bridget," he said, not daring to take his eyes off his screen.

"Hello, Austin." I couldn't help but think how ironic it was that he had the same name as my brother. He was sweet and his life had been hard, marked as it was by numerous foster families.

"I'm sorry about your brother," he said and finally turned his head toward me. He looked like a punished dog, and I felt as if I was the one who had punished him.

"It's okay," I said. "You didn't do anything." I didn't get why people apologized. If it wasn't their fault, why be sorry? Maybe they had a loss of words? Maybe they were uncomfortable? Whatever it was, when someone apologized to me, I always responded with, "You didn't do anything."

For the rest of the class, we did our work in silence. During our break, I went to the counselor's office. He was a fit man who had attended high school with my dad. There was a round table in the center of the room with soft chairs that made you want to curl up in them. I went in to see him merely to avoid the people in the hallways. I had no intention of talking to him, especially since he always asked how my day was going, a question that seemed hopelessly rhetorical.

Over the days that followed, I made a habit of going to the counselor's office during break and lunch since my classmates seemed unsure about what to say or do around me. There seemed no reason to be social, and I rarely answered questions in class or talked to the person next to me. Teachers and staff were concerned, which resulted in more visits to the counselor's office. The more time I spent there, the harder it was to wean myself from the comfort of that sanctuary.

Some days, I didn't even bother going to the counselor's office. I would just go outside or hang out in the restroom. No one asked where I was supposed to be. My teachers figured I was in the office. I was never confronted for ditching classes. Usually, I sat peacefully and played games on my phone to distract me from things I didn't want to think about. I ditched because I couldn't handle being around people who felt they had to be guarded around me and treated me as if I was different or breakable.

One day, I was sitting outside the school, hiding by a pillar. The highway was in front of me, and behind it, an open field. I still remember the feeling that came over me. I wanted to run and be free. I wanted to lay on my back in the field as if I had nothing to worry about.

December 12, 2008 was my thirteenth birthday. Thirteen days after Austin's death was how I remembered it. I didn't want a big celebration, but my mom and grandma thought it was important. All of my friends and classmates were invited to go bowling. Afterwards,

Sandy and my family would have a nice dinner at the steakhouse. I recall the day like it was written on paper. My mom picked all of us up from school, and we drove to the bowling alley and ate pizza. The car ride was twenty minutes, but it went by quickly. For the first time in two weeks, I felt happy. I forgot everything. I imagined this was how it felt like for someone high on ecstasy. It was then I decided my goal was to forget.

At the bowling alley, a peculiar thing happened. I talked to Sheri, one of the girls I disliked, as if she were my friend. I have no idea what came over me. Maybe it was my good mood, or I was actually enjoying her company. Still, I had mood swings, and I struggled to transition from one to the next. By the end of the day, I was exhausted.

After dinner at the steakhouse, my family returned to my grandparents' house where I opened my presents, many of which were from family and friends. "Just because my brother died doesn't mean I need twenty journals, Mom," I complained. "I'm doing fine, it's quite obvious." Mom told me to be grateful anyways and to thank everyone for their thoughtfulness. Still, I took offense at getting all those journals, convinced as I was that I was doing fine.

One day before Christmas break, I requested that all of Austin's friends meet me in the office so I could talk to them about how they were doing. I don't know why I cared, but I often found that my mind wasn't functioning correctly, as if I were bipolar. They told me they were taking everything one step at a time and embracing their memories of Austin. Then they each told me how they had found out about Austin's death, which helped me get out of my own world.

Sometimes, I would be proud when someone honored Austin. Other times, I raged when someone had the audacity to disrupt my mental block of Austin. My family and friends were guarded around me because they never knew how I would react moment to moment.

My brain was scrambling, like I had no idea I was making decisions. I just acted and spoke without thinking. My life was running at a fast pace, and I couldn't keep up with it.

One day, I snapped when I saw a binder that belonged to one of the girls I didn't like. It said "RIP Austin." Without thinking, I demanded, "Who do you think you are? Don't you ever think about the other people around you who have to see that? He was my brother. I'm more sensitive about it than you think." The tears rolled down my burning face. I had always been the girl she could push around and step on. For once, I was in control. She reacted with shock, mouth open as she tried to find the right words. With my fists balled up, I walked away.

Until that moment, I hadn't known I had the nerve to stand up and say what was on my mind. I felt powerful, not like a bully, but like a stronger person. For the first time in a long time, I began to feel like I had my hands on the wheel and could steer my life in the direction I wanted it to go. I believed I had a good reason to act out and that I didn't have to explain why the binder had bothered me. After all, everyone understood why I was never in class.

The support group at my church met once a week and the more we met, the more it seemed to transform into a group more interested in complaining than healing. Many of the teenage girls from my school came ready to backstab friends and cause problems. It became less about my brother's death and more about people getting even with one another. I started going less and less and began to despise some of the girls. Because they weren't talking about my brother anymore, I took it as disrespect for him. The leader said that it was their way of grieving, though I believed everyone in that room knew it was the perfect opportunity to betray one another.

My parents had bought me a book that gave 50 tips for grieving children. I childrenI opened it. I was only interested in one out of the 50: getting a dog. I have had a couple of dogs in my life, but none recently. Soon enough, I had a baby boy Australian Shepherd in my arms every night before I went to sleep.

With each passing day, my town seemed less welcoming. I heard stories of someone's wife cheating with someone's husband. The ugly rumors touched our lives as well. Once, my uncle was in the tractor store and someone pulled him aside and said he had seen his wife on a boat on the lake with another man. He described him as "a short, burly man." The man happened to be my father who was my aunt's cousin. Worse, there were rumors spreading left and right about how my brother died. Even though his death was on the front page on every newspaper in Nothern Nevada, rumors persisted. My family and I were beginning to believe it was time for a new town. A truly clean start.

LOOKING BACK...

There were a lot of triggers and reminders of Austin's death. In my generation, kids use suicide as a joke. They say things like, "Oh, I'm so bored I want to kill myself." Of course, before we lost Austin, this never really phased me. After all I have gone through since his death, I never find these comments or "jokes" funny. When I had the courage, I would say, "My brother committed suicide." That always shut them up. If I was watching a movie that depicted a suicide—or even a death—my heart would pound a mile a minute and heat would wash over me. I would disengage my brain from that movie and try to find a happy thought or something to distract me so I wouldn't cry.

Even at school there were many triggers. Once I was put on the spot during writing class. We were to write about a life experience that had changed us. Several in my class complained that they had no idea what to write about. Our teacher said, "Write about something like what Bridget went through when her brother died." I don't think he realized that not everyone has found their brother dead at a young age or lost someone close to them. Sandy had told me that her health class teacher had given a lesson on suicide and death. Though my parents offered to send a professional to teach the class or arrange for the counselor to assist, the principal declined and the teacher ended up doing the week-long lesson on her own. She compared her dad's death to Austin's, which upset the class. It was a shame that no one at my school wanted to get the students the proper help they needed.

hurdles

Three weeks after Austin's death, we moved back into our old house, and it was haunted with memories. The once familiar home didn't seem like my home anymore. There was an absent feeling deep inside me, like when you know you forgot something or forgot to say something. It's on the tip of your tongue, but not close enough to fully grasp. Something was missing, and without that something, my home was simply a house. The smell was different too—like the smell of a new car. But it was more than just the new carpet, new paint, and new doors. Whatever it was, it made me feel uncomfortable and reluctant to adapt to my surroundings. I walked through the house, letting my eyes wander from every trinket to every floorboard. My body was stiff, as if bracing for the worst. Though I didn't dare step foot in my parents' room, the other familiar rooms I entered made me flinch as if something might jump out at me. For every step forward I took, I forced my memory to take one step back. To guard against memories I didn't want to revisit, I created my own delete button.

I didn't relax there for days. I would see Austin in the house, and though I knew it was the result of my imagination—of longing and wanting him with me—I felt crazy. Even though our Christmas tree was set up in the living room, it wasn't comforting. There were no memories of decorating it or putting up the star. I did appreciate the people who put it up for us, but it wasn't the same. Of course, nothing would ever be the same.

Merry Christmas and Happy Holidays! Love, The Park Family
Our Family Christmas card many years ago.

That year we didn't send out a Christmas card. With moving back into our house and grieving, there wasn't time, let alone the desire to make time. We all knew Christmas would be hard, so on Christmas Eve we all laid in my parents' big comfy bed. It was the second time I had ventured into my parents' room since Austin's death. Christmas movies were on the television, but I was fixated on the snow falling outside. I reminisce on those moments when I was calm and happy. Every Christmas Eve, excitement made it difficult for me to fall asleep, and that year it was the same. Since my parents refused to tell me what we were doing for the Christmas holiday, my mind fluttered with all the possibilities of the days to follow. Regardless, I knew that whatever happened, we would all feel an absence.

The next morning, I woke up alone to a lot of snow. In Nevada, especially near the mountains, snow is always expected on Christmas. I jumped off the big bed and walked into the living room, hoping to see all the presents and family. Instead, I saw that my parents were dressed for Mass. They were drinking their coffee and there were no presents. I couldn't help but think, "Just because Austin's gone doesn't mean we can't have fun." Fortunately, I knew how to censor my mouth (somewhat) back then.

I said "Good morning," with as much delight as I could muster. Still, my parents read the expression on my face.

"Bridget, why don't you look through your stocking?" my mom said.

My stocking was made of traditional red and white felt. It hung on the railing by the tree. As I neared, my excitement shot up. When I reached inside, there was something made of material. I pulled it out, and in my hand were leis.

"What do you think those are for, Bridget?"

My parents always made me think. They never could just tell me what I wanted to know. It was then I recalled reading my mom's email from a few days earlier. It had said something about Hawaii.

I guessed correctly, and my mom said, "We are leaving in a few days. Your Aunt Carrie, Kassy, Terry, and all your cousins are coming too. But today, after Mass, we're going to Aunt Carrie's to eat and go sledding!"

Mass seemed to last forever, but when it was finally over, we were on our way. The drive took about two hours because of the amount of snow.

My cousins were all years younger than me, with the exception of Kristen who was only six months younger. My aunt's house is in the mountains, and it is a cozy cabin. As soon as we opened the door, various smells invigorated me. This was my favorite time of year.

After hours of sledding, dinner was finally ready. We ate turkey, elk, potatoes, pie, stuffing, yams, and gravy.

My grandpa volunteered to say grace, and we all joined hands and bowed our heads. "God, thank you for all you have blessed us with. Thank you for giving me my family and to have us all here. Keep Austin in all of our hearts. Amen." There were tears in his eyes when he lifted his head.

I felt stiff and awkward, like he had spoken unspeakable words. It ruined my happiness, and so I deleted my thoughts and moved on. I learned to do this easily.

My cousin and I talked about all we had been going through. We grew up together and knew each other like we were twins. We had a bond, but it wasn't the same as what Austin and I had shared. Her parents were divorced, and her dad and my mom were both struggling with the loss we all suffered. She felt caught in the middle, as if responsible for supporting and showing love to each of her parents. I felt bad for her. We ended that subject and moved on to talk about the trip to Hawaii. We were both excited. It was our first big family vacation together.

When I got home that night, I went with my dad to see if the horse trailer lights would work. We hooked up the trailer. The lights turned on so brightly that it reminded me of the light in Austin's eyes whenever he laughed. I decided it was a sign from God that he was okay and happy. Later, I lay in my bed with the blinds closed and the covers pulled over my head, wondering what the rest of my life would bring.

During the plane ride to Hawaii, I thought about how fortunate my family was to have a house and each other. I didn't feel like a victim when I put myself in that state of mind. Still, I could never make up my mind how to feel. If I was sad, I would make myself be happy. But I never felt complete. Grieving wasn't an option.

On the island, we hiked up a volcano and left one of Austin's bracelets there in honor and remembrance of him. In pursuit of happiness, we enjoyed the vacation, but we missed Austin.

There was a constant struggle for me to adjust to my new life. I was acting out. I came into contact with people I didn't want to associate with. Some were Austin's friends. Others were kids at my school who felt like they had to talk to me. Most friendships were good, but there was a bad one. I confided in one of Austin's friends and it proved to be a bad choice. I had entered into an emotional relationship that I thought would comfort me, but in the end, it only exposed me to verbal and emotional abuse. To sum it up, I learned a lesson.

In February, three months following Austin's death, his birthday rolled around. He would have been fifteen. He and my dad share the same birthday. My mom tells the story that when she was giving birth to Austin, she let my dad watch Monday night football in honor of his own birthday. My dad and Austin had an incredible bond. They always seemed to know what the other was thinking.

We celebrated both birthdays that day, but none of us enjoyed it. My dad's birthday had always revolved around Austin. Whether Austin was going to have friends over or go to the park, my dad always blew out his candles in private and let Austin enjoy their day.

Without Austin there, all the attention was focused on my dad. The atmosphere in the room was drab and depressing. My mom and I had bought a cake and presents, hoping to still celebrate his birth. I was disappointed that my dad didn't enjoy his day as I would have liked.

People will let you down, intentionally or otherwise. They either do something of which you disapprove or don't do something and let you down. My dad often said, "Damned if you do, damned if you don't." It seemed like whatever he said, there would come a time when it made sense.

I began to feel like I could not please my parents. The absent feeling in our home made it a house, and the missing person in our family made roommates out of those of us who had been left behind. Every night, the cold silence outside my room would sweep in under my door to haunt me.

I would pray to God, apologizing for doubting Him and asking for help and forgiveness, for my family was not the same. I felt as if my parents were so depressed that there was nothing I could do. I became a hellion, a rebel. I skipped school and was infatuated with an older boy. I had a temper. But I could never admit I was the one making my parents the way they were. I reasoned with myself, saying: "This is how you are grieving, so let it take its course." But grieving isn't about making conscious mistakes and acting out. I had some self-awareness and yet no self control.

In March, after a long day of school, my mother drove me home from volleyball practice. "Bridget," she said, "I think I found something that would help you, if you want."

I looked out the window and noticed that the snow knew how to perfectly cover each hill and mountain. It was like smooth frosting on a cake.

"It's for grief support," my mom continued. "You remember Julie, don't you?" Julie was my aunt's ex-husband's sister. She was a therapist and a mother of teenagers, which made me feel better.

"Sounds great, Mom." No harm, no foul, I thought. I knew, subconsciously, that I had faults and that she might be able to help me.

Julie did help. However, when my parents got involved, it was hell. I told Julie that I thought I was depressed and that I was concerned about my parents. I also confessed that a boy was controlling me, and I didn't know how to escape the relationship.

The next day after school, I sat in the cafeteria with the friend of the older boy I was seeing. "I don't know what it is or why it is," I told her, "but I'm just not happy." I hoped she would offer some sort of solution.

"Bridget, is he a healthy person for you to be with?" Kyla was such a beautiful girl with brown eyes and warm hair that lit up her tan skin.

"Well, he does help me a lot." I always covered for him and avoided tipping the conversation toward the verbal abuse to which he subjected me. He would call me nasty words, then apologize and say he would never let me go. "I am just not feeling the way I think I should. I wish my life was the same as it was six months ago. I know there is nothing I can change, but I just wish I was at peace! My life isn't fulfilling, and I sometimes wish it was over." With every word I spoke, I felt my blood rush through me. The more I thought about it, the more I felt weak and distraught.

When my parents picked me up from school, I felt the silence in the car and knew something was wrong. "Dad, are you okay?" I could tell by his solemn look that something was terribly wrong.

"You know what you did, Bridget," he said.

My mind flipped through my day, trying to land on something that would solve this riddle.

"Did you talk to Kyla today?" he asked. I looked down and nodded. I knew I was in trouble, but I didn't know why. When we arrived home, I recalled the conversation Kyla and I had earlier that day—and knew I was in trouble.

When we walked in our house, my mom asked, "Bridget do you really feel this way?"

I had no idea how to answer this question honestly. During dinner, I tried to recall more of my conversation with Kayla, but like much of my life, I had blocked it out.

LOOKING BACK...

Have you ever had a dream, then you woke up feeling like it was real and had really happened? That's how my life was. I'd wake up from a great dream of my family of four, or of a dream of Austin and think that my brother was sleeping in the room next to mine. Of course, he wasn't.

I am lucky that my brother was honored in so many ways. His graduating class received sweatshirts with his name printed on them, and in Douglas where we had lived before moving to Smith Valley, a group called A.S.P.I.R.E made a memorial for all the teens who had died in our area. Austin was included, and his football #22 was painted in orange. There was a nice ceremony to reveal the memorial, and I made friends with other girls who had lost a brother. The memorial is located at the local middle school and is surrounded by a beautiful garden. I feel fortunate to be able to see it from the side of the road when I drive past it.

normalcy

A prayer that helps me now, and which I wish I had known when everything changed in our lives is the Serenity Prayer. It helped me to pray about what I needed to change, what I couldn't change, and to have the wisdom to know the difference. I didn't realize that this was my new life, and that one day, I would have to accept it and accept myself. I went from hiding in sweatshirts and baggy pants to wearing makeup and being fashionable.

Still, I grew up too fast, uncertain of the outcome. I thought I needed to mature so I could be accepted. Sometimes it felt as if nothing could possibly go right and that my life was a constant struggle. If I wasn't struggling, I was neither happy nor sad. I wasn't living. I was just alive...

My parents did the right thing when my school counselor called them and told them about my conversation with Kyla that day. They feared the loss of their remaining child. I don't blame them. I hurt them when I told them I was depressed. I hurt them when I told them I wasn't happy. I never felt so low, but I had to get it off my chest.

My parents reacted normally by taking away my phone and keeping me close at all times. At night, I slept in their room, and if I was in the shower, they would check on me. It annoyed me, but I don't blame them now for worrying.

A few days after the conversation with Kyla, my parents took me for a mental health checkup. It frightened me to think I might be bipolar or mentally disturbed. In the waiting room, I was nervous, and I felt the tension between my parents and me. To this day, when I feel this tension, I hate it. Just the thought of my parents being mad or disappointed in me is upsetting.

The atmosphere of the office was depressing. The walls were wooden and there were cliché pictures of trees and meadows. When my name was called, a man with a moustache and spectacles took me into an office. It had a sofa and a desk with one chair in front of it. There was very little lighting, and the room gave off a feeling of uncertainty. We all knew why I was depressed. I was heartbroken with my new life. That, on top of losing my brother, made me feel like a lost little girl. I thought I was older than what I was. I thought I was mature. I thought I could handle anything and everything. "Bring on the questions," I said over and over in my head.

I don't know how or when I got over this phase in my life, but it was an uphill battle. My therapy with Julie helped me rebuild a strong foundation for me and my parents. When possible, we all attended the sessions together. If one parent couldn't go, I always had the other with me. We talked about Austin and how we were all coping, then we discussed my behavioral issues. I realized that I was making my parents deal with a lot at once. I added to the pain and suffering they had been experiencing since the loss of their beloved son. Once I understood that, we reached the same level of trust for the first time in a while. Once everything attained a new "normal," I was able to sleep in my own room and take showers without interruptions.

Later, I joined a group that was for families who have lost a loved one through death or divorce. It was a two-hour drive to Solace Tree. The small brick house with its small lawn was located in the hood behind the university and near the casinos. When I walked across the street, I saw needles and tubes. It scared me.

Inside that little brick house, there were artwork on the walls, canvases, and furniture. In each room, there were either toddlers, children, teenagers, or adults. When my mom dropped me off at the teen room, she looked at me with promise in her eyes.

The walls in the room were wooden, just like at the mental health office. There were about eight kids in the room, and later I would learn that each had his or her own story. All eyes were on me.

"No pressure, Bridget," said a lady who wore a Solace Tree shirt. "Find a seat and you'll be okay." She looked around. "I'd like to thank you all for coming. I know for some of you it's hard, too."

After that, she went over the rules. The ones I remember most clearly were: "You don't have to share," "Everything stays confidential," and "Respect others' thoughts."

The lady's name was Sarah, and she had lost her dad when she was younger. "Now we will go around the room," she said, "and if you'd like to share about your loss, we'd like for you to do so."

I heard stories of illness, accidents, murders, and suicides. I thought about how if you look deep look into someone's eyes, you can sometimes see sorrow. But there's more mystery behind it all. Some kids cried and some smiled while talking about their lost loved one. Some were emotionless.

When it was my turn, I said; "I'm Bridget, I'm from a small town, and I lost my brother to suicide." I braced myself to hear "I'm sorry" a million more times. Instead, everyone asked questions about him. "How old was he? Were you guys close? What sports did he play?" It was refreshing, and my anxiety began to recede. For once, there was no pity. There was compassion.

Later that night, I paid a visit to Austin's website. Even now when I go on it, I have mixed emotions that include happiness, guilt, and confusion. I also experience a sense of love. People I have never met know about the loss that my parents and I suffered.

I clicked on the "memories" link, and the most recent memory was from one of Austin's ex-girlfriends. She wrote:

> *"I will never forget all the good times with you. There have been so many. I remember when we went to a basketball game in Reno and you were practicing your "mating call" on all the ladies. Then we went to a buffet and you made me eat all this weird exotic food like swordfish, oysters and clams. Hahaha. And when we went to your house and you were showing off on the trampoline and you did a flip and hit your foot on the ceiling of your shed. That was funny. I remember on our way to Yerington for AO (Academic Olympics) when Mrs. Francois got pulled over for speeding and the second the cop left you said "smooth" like a smart alec. AND you didn't have your seatbelt on when we got pulled over! We've had some good times. One of my favorite memories was when we were dating and I came to your house for New Year's. You showed off for me the whole night. First, your dad said he doubted you could eat one of those jalapenos so you stuffed one in your mouth, acting all cool and a second later you were at the sink drinking water out of the hose because it was so hot. Lol. And when we were in*

the hot tub and you got out and acted all cool but then you slipped and fell on the ice. I really miss all the good times with Austin but he will be in my heart forever. I love and miss you so much."

I remembered that New Year's Eve. I kept trying to separate Austin and his girlfriend in the hot tub because I was immature and didn't like any girl that liked him. More memories flooded me, and I began to type.

"A memory I treasure with my brother was last year at the Celebrity Golf Tournament. We (Sandy, Me, Austin, Thomas, and Sol) were at dinner in the club-house. We were really bored and decided to walk around. We went downstairs and we found the celebrity locker room. Sandy and Austin just walked in the room and was snooping through all of the lockers! Of course, Sol, Thomas and I stayed behind to watch these insane and stupid people do that. Then we heard 3 loud voices and we ran up the stairs leaving Austin and Sandy behind. They ran into the showers and kept quiet. In the room, there were 3 celebrities. One of them was Charles Barkley. They stayed quiet till they saw the 3 figures leave the room. I will always remember that fun memory with my brother!!"

I then scrolled to the "Condolences" screen and came across this from "a mom":

"While looking to find what day of the week my daughter was born on (She was born on Feb. 22, 1994.) I found this website. I noticed the dates of precious Austin's life. He has my Sarah's birthday exactly and

my husband's birthday as his Home going to Heaven. I cannot imagine the sorrow. Having read many of the" Condolences" that others have posted, I have found myself drawn to this family. New prayers are with you this day. May God bless you and continue to restore your peace."

It amazed me that people I didn't know prayed for us. It made me think of the happiness as well as the sorrow that the date of November 29th brings to this woman and her daughter. I returned the favor and prayed for this mom.

My life may not be the same as it was five years ago, but how I get through the day, the week, or even the hour is by accepting how I feel and not being discouraged about it. There came a time when I ceased wearing black and I began to see glimpses of my old self again. I felt almost a sense of relief when my rosary broke and with it, my vow to never take it off. It was as if I could finally let go of my past and grudges. I grieve accordingly and have found myself happier in the long run. A quote that best honors my brother is "Loved by many, forgotten by none."

I think of my life now as if I'm still learning from the mistakes I made then, yet I am growing as a person, continuously. When my life was dark, I felt as if it would always be so. I may have been forced to mature fast at a young age, but I truly felt I was growing young. My life was rushed when I was young, urged to be strong. I feel as if I missed three years of my life when I was grieving.

I lived in Smith Valley until the middle of my freshmen year in high school. Before I started my freshmen year, my parents and I thought it would be great to host a foreign exchange student to give me company and a friend in the house. We read over the expectations that we would treat her like family. She would call me her sister and address my parents as mom and dad. She was expected to be treated as equally as I was. We pondered the idea for a while, then put our plan into place. The summer before Austin died, we had hosted a French exchange student and he had been great and became a lifelong friend. This time, we chose a Spanish girl who was one year older than me. Her name was Sola. We felt obligated to tell her the situation about my brother and worried that she wouldn't accept our family. But she and her family offered condolences and agreed to the exchange. Until the day Sola arrived, we chatted with her online and told her about where we lived.

We waited for her plane to arrive at 9:00 at night, along with another family that was also hosting a girl from Spain. Every person who walked out of her gate, we would always ask each other if it was her. When she finally walked out, I gave her a big hug, but she didn't hug back. She had a full set of bangs, round brown eyes, and a long face.

The next morning I had volleyball practice but Sola watched because she had jet lag. By becoming a part of a small school, the exchange students were expected to play as soon as possible. I was so excited to finally have her there, but she acted as if she wasn't excited at all. During the whole practice, she was either on her cell phone, which she was not allowed to have, or sleeping.

Over lunch, we had to break it to Sola that the company her exchange is with doesn't allow their students to have unlimited access to cell phones or any social networking sites. All she had was one hour a week to use the computer to socialize with family back home. I guess her parents left it to us to tell her because she had no idea. "Sola," my mom started, "the rules state that you are only allowed one hour per week to communicate back home." Sola looked up from her food and said, "If I would've known that, I wouldn't have come here." Then she continued to stab her food angrily with her fork, shocking me and my mom.

Five months later, we had the final straw and we figured out she was not screened well when she was accepted into the exchange program. What could have been a beautiful experience, lifelong friendship, and a potential sister figure turned out to be the opposite. We did everything we could to prepare for her stay and keep her happy but Sola never really wanted the experience we did.

In the middle of my freshman year, our family moved to Reno which is over an hour drive from Smith Valley. I transferred to a private Catholic school, though not because I needed to be "fixed" or was in trouble. I was enrolled so that I could be surrounded by peers who shared my faith.

The first day at my new school was frightening. The campus and student population were ten times the size of my previous school. Fortunately, I did know some of the students, and they were kind enough to guide me. It was odd to see crosses over every door and a chapel across from the cafeteria, but I liked it. I adjusted well to the school uniforms, school Masses, and daily prayers.

It was awkward when people asked if I had siblings. I simply said, "I am an only child," or "My brother died in 2008." No one really knew how to react, especially since I didn't give them the expected answer that I did, in fact, have a sibling.

It was hard for me to make friends in the beginning since I came in the middle of the second semester and the students had already formed their cliques. Sometimes at lunch I would sit by my locker and eat alone because I had no one to sit with. When people asked if I wanted to join them, I thought they did it out of pity.

I continued to attend counseling sessions at Solace Tree with my mom, and once we moved to Reno, we decided it was our turn to help others who had suffered the loss of a loved one. We went through training and were certified as group facilitators.

I found that I was able to relate to other teens in my group because we were equal in age. When I was having a bad day or thought I had it bad, I reminded myself of some of the teens in my group and how they probably had it worse than I did.

Following Austin's death, our family set up a scholarship in my brother's name that was awarded to a graduate from Smith Valley. My family and I went to the school and I presented the scholarship at the awards ceremony and announced the recipient(s). It was always odd going back to my old school, particularly since some of the students thought that because I had moved and now attended a private school I must believe I was "too good" for them. It wasn't like that at all.

looking forward

Over the years, I have stayed in contact with a few of my friends from Smith Valley, and today my best friend is Anne. Though we were peers and friends while I lived in Smith Valley, it wasn't until Sandy and I drifted apart that Anne and I formed the incredible bond that lasts to this day. She sometimes comes to Reno to stay with my family or join us for dinner. She always remembers to call me on Austin's birthday or death anniversary to see how I'm coping.

Once I began to steadily improve and accept that grieving is normal, I stopped seeing Julie. Still, there are nights when I cry for my brother or for no reason at all. It's as if, in suppressing my feelings for as long as I did, I created a reservoir of emotion deep inside me. At times, it simply needs a release, even to the point of overflowing. Afterwards, I always feel relief.

My mom revealed to me a few months ago that she has been talking to a psychic (who speaks of God as the only god) who has helped her cope with the loss of Austin for the past three years. She decided to finally tell me because I was talking about how badly I wanted to talk to a psychic. Later on, this same lady spoke with my dad on a few occasions and he had a positive experience.

During my first conversation with this woman, I wasn't sure if what she claimed to be able to do was real, but she gave me signs that only my brother and I would know that could validate his presence. She told me that Austin said to "watch out for cars and to save money." She had no idea what this meant and neither did I until a few months later when I was backing up my car and hit my mom's car so severely that I had to pay for the damages. I wish I would have saved my money…

I often reflect on my conversations with this woman that she recorded and gave to me. Though, in the beginning, I didn't know for certain that what she claimed to be able to do was real, I now believe it is and she has helped me in so many ways.

I now know I suffer with nightmares and anxiety, not only from Austin's death, but from a boat incident that happened a few years back when a friend of mine lost a few toes and from the abusive relationship I was involved in. I experience anxiety and nightmares almost every night and some of the nightmares are recurring ones. I lay in bed and worry about things that will happen in years to come. When I awaken from these nightmares, I have flashbacks of finding my brother or my friend bleeding in the water. Every day, I am tired from the lack of sleep or the emotional stress.

I get paranoid if I'm expecting to hear from someone and I don't. I fear that something bad has happened to them. I stay away from movies or situations that might offend me or cause pain, especially those that feature or reference suicide.

Though there was a time I felt as if I was truly crazy, I now know I can't help how I am and that I must take one day at a time. I learned that I would rather have a good day than cause myself to have a bad day because I don't want to feel crazy.

This is my story, so far. I never expected to experience tragedy at such a young age, and I know I will face other hurdles in life. Still, I believe I will overcome whatever lands in my path—one hurdle at a time.

My hopes are to share my story nationwide and to motivate others by speaking engagements. I aspire to write more books and share my story throughout the upcoming years. I now surround myself with healthy, positive people.

Me, at my junior prom, with my dog, Rudy. Credits: Molly Park and makeup by Silvia Cabrera.

Me my junior year along with one of my best friends and Co- cheer captain.

REFERENCES

If you are ever considering suicide, please use these resources below and learn that your life is valuable.

www.yourlifeyourchoice.com

www.contactwecare.org

www.suicidehotlines.com

www.solacetree.org

National Suicide Prevention Lifeline 1-800-273-8255

The Power to Prevent Suicide: A Guide for Teens Helping Teens by Richard E. Nelson

When Nothing Matters Anymore: A Survival Guide for Depressed Teens by Bev Cobain

You can also take a pledge to seek help for hurting yourself.

www.samhsa.gov/ppreventionweek/pledge

appendix

WHERE TO GO FOR HELP

There are a lot of resources for someone who is suffering a loss such as books, the internet, and therapy. There are also support groups in your area.

BOOKS THAT YOU ALSO MIGHT HAVE INTEREST IN...

My Son..My Son...A Guide to Healing by Iris Bolten
Do They Have Bad Days in Heaven? by Michelle Lynn-Quat
Healing Your Grieving Heat: 100 Practical Ideas by Alan D. Wolfelt, PH.D.
Surving the Death of a Sibling by T.J. Wray

about the author

BRIDGET PARK

Born and raised in the great state of Nevada, she now hopes to inspire with her story and encourage those to grieve healthily and to always remember our lost loved ones. This is her first book and plans to continue writing during college and to progressively continue to share more of her inspirational story.

Made in the USA
San Bernardino, CA
23 November 2013